NO ROĄ ____ ᴍᴇ

The enormous journey of guilt

SEVENTY-EIGHT POEMS

Writing No.15

No Road Home

First Published in 2024
by Peter Hague – Concept – Design – Art Direction

ISBN 978-1-7394388-2-1

Cover Design, layout, typography and cover art:
Peter Hague Concept Design Art Direction.
Photography: ©PeterHague 1972-2023

Also available in hardback: **ISBN** 978-1-7394388-3-8

A catalogue record for this book
is available from the British Library.

Copies of all my books are held at The Bodleian Library Oxford University, the Cambridge University Library, National Library of Scotland, National Library of Wales and Trinity College Dublin for Legal Deposit.

www.peterhague.com

NO ROAD HOME

The enormous journey of guilt

SEVENTY-EIGHT POEMS

Winifred
David and John
Lara

Judith

"We are lost, you and I, in the deep seats of our lives –

pinned back and helpless,

as time rushes through our ever-closer stations.

It is time measured by design and desire,

and in the shortening tracks of a limited future –

cast in whims that briefly register

on the harassed pile of today's schedule.

Thus we ingratiate our whitewashed lives

with the implications of a reconcilable past.

There is a discipline of waiting too –

an eternity of wanting things to be right –

but also blessed and true,

in that casual blur of distracted longing."

from 'Ever-closer Stations: A lament'

AN INTRODUCTION BY THE AUTHOR

2024

The foundation of this book is built on poems that are often directly written as welcome affirmations of the painful struggle that we may all find ourselves facing, should we slip through the boundaries of their difficult truths. They are welcome via their attempts at understanding the various dilemmas at their core – the situations and emotional conditions that have us lost and wandering in an existential maze. As an initial proposition, I can say that much of this book, though somewhat semi-autobiographical, not only deals with the important details that form the various entanglements of lives, it tends to deal with them in terms of their place in the wider picture and sometimes in abstract and creative ways and from different viewpoints.

So this book is a broad examination of displacement, loneliness, loyalty, guilt, despair, misconduct, delinquency, liability, disgrace, regret, responsibility, shame, dereliction and penitence. And apart from that burden which is delivered by our own actions, intended or otherwise, it is also an examination of the frustration we may feel when other forces, people or institutions, do things which cause ourselves or others to bear some affliction or suffering that they do not deserve.

An example of this second proposition can be witness by the current batch of unqualified world leaders and peripheral billionaires, who seem content to effect our lives in ways they have little or no mandate for, while arrogantly insisting they know the way forward, having already lead us to the open gates of this unsettled era of turmoil and insecurity. To this end, they have the bamboozled majority unhappily countenanced in blind servitude – unable to take back the constitutional control of the respective foundations of the various communities. Meanwhile, our values, our safety factors and our general stability, are all being thrown into the waste bin of global disaffection without the channels for effective protest. The usurpers will fail of course, but at great cost to the embedded strength of our various trusted systems. They have set many of our communities to smoulder under that quiet fire of division, racism and mistrust. It is an engineered negativity that undeniably dominates our brutally reshaped lives.

These broken institutions have also been attacked by the overtly liberal media, which seems to function now only as a proper-gander machine, tirelessly motivated by agenda-shaped bulletins. These are seemingly delivered by a cabal of specially chosen employees, all working to carry out the bidding of some unseen tyrant-messiah of woke. This is another machine-like entity, whose disciples are the 'activists of anything', those self-proclaimed warriors who guide misled future comrades towards the seething fires of largely hatred-based identity politics and call it a crusade for 'justice'. In truth, these driven fools often have no idea of what they are supporting – and those who do – are best avoided. They are dark and dangerous mercenaries, often righteously arrogant and standing on what could be described as, the far-right side of left – pulling the strings of the new proletariat – the new nazi jackboot you won't see coming; a truth hidden behind the soft shoes of Doctor Zhivago.

The human race is more tribal than some people are willing to admit – but there is nothing wrong with that – the world loves to fly its flags. The struggle of integration became the weak hope of diversity, and the pride of a balanced civilisation was cast into the often misleading gutter of modernist deconstruction. The conceptual hope of a safe and stabilising legacy is almost becoming a hate crime now, and filled out by the floundering quiet of new forms of revenge-based racism and pigeon-holing.

From such a position, there is no road home for the families of earth, only new battlefields coloured with blood and bureaucracy. And while these bigger events are in progress, there is no thought of healing those smaller issues of personal detail for the necessary well-being of individual lives – and therefore the health of communities. It seems that people are no longer permitted to exist in their own right, they now have to be a small part of the homogenous many, via a crudely-labelled, almost off-the-peg 'identity' – as sanctioned by the sprawl of idealist experiments in social bonding and reordering. And they can no longer declare themselves as individuals, because they soon become lost in the bigger picture of a chaotic world; a heavy-handed cynicism of slave consumerism and vice, the devil in the detail that defeats every little voice – those talking to God moments, in the spirit of night, when the world is still and we are each surrounded by the hope of nothingness and by the fear of hell, both realities sharing the same moment in a negotiation for peace.

CONTENTS

1
Lost Lands

2
A Recommended Heart

3
What Strangers Know

CONTENTS

4
The Sea Takes Me Home

5
Late in the Day

6
Apocalypse of Poverty or Just Me?

NO ROAD HOME

The enormous journey of guilt

"But I have promises to keep,
And miles to go before I sleep..."

Robert Frost

1
PART ONE

Lost Lands

A King with One Eye

Attempting to explain my dubious heart.

Life is trying to kill me – let it –
let it go that unoriginal way,
while I plant a second seed in the wrong furrow
and catch an arrow in my second eye.
The seed is one of universal grace,
that grows my legend – beyond heir apparent.
To be crowned the king of pain is one thing,
but to be scorned as King of ruthless verse?
I will spend my days listening to courtiers
attempting to explain my dubious heart.
Let them – O let them try to kill me,
I was dead from the second I inherited this thought.

Sew my poems into your careful walls,
or into the furrows of your loyal heart.
They will grow like poppies in the blistered braille
of all the half-blind battles fought.

It is a clumsy elegance that might survive
my stupid, one-eyed, unfocussed death,
when autumn leaves will lay like shields
on a blind coffin of murdered breath.
They will blow across your comet's path –
a godly horn, delaying sleep, or even rest.

A POLITICAL LURCH TOWARDS APOLOGY

A place where I can tempt public indifference.

I want to be a politician and live amongst the people.
I do not want an office in Westminster –
just a pavement with cracks and leaves
and the wind blowing through inexpensive words.
A place where I can tempt public indifference –
to question their reliance on blatant liars.
"Listen," I will say, "you have lost almost everything
by paying attention to mere effigies of leaders –
following their path over the parapet of war,
as they use your precious lives for their own cover."

Tell them, in your own dead voice,
to cease representing complex desires.
Tell them, it is they who have no choice.

And do not form an unexpected queue to my paradise;
I cannot cure your political ills with any sound advice –
nor with words approaching comfort, truth or faith –
only the single value offered by love –
and that is fidelity – the child of grace.
                It was a surprise to me too,
but I cannot help you breathe above the surface of politics.
I am only here today, amongst your submerged hearts,
to say I have nothing left to explain, or teach,
but for some reason, I want to tell you everything –
everything I cannot possibly know or even reach.

TRIBUTARIES OF THE SEA OF BLOOD

A voice that seems the same as mine.

I have studied poetry and its many lines,
but have not travelled far
into its rivers of veins.
My own life is too short
to hear the echoes of new shores –
so I drift on this tide of words and their remains;
on the breathing waves of mutual influence –
turning, toward the next true thought.
A voice that seems the same as mine,
yet is different still, and came this way,
without my reasons or my will.

A SURPLUS OF LIGHT ENTERTAINMENT

We humans don't care enough to need a planet.

It is too late to save the world;
it has chosen to die of its own ignorance.
You can see that on television every day,
with the endless spillings of its childish stars.
We humans don't care enough to need a planet –
we need only a world of lurid spite.
Its entertainment will exist beyond our threshold –
as it moves out into space –
and a long day – called night.

THE CURTAIN OF SAND

He is the curtain of life that lives in waves.

Let us go down to the monstrous sea,
where every wave-splash is a celebration –
not of joy, but in the burial of the past.

Let the monstrosity play its hand,
to that thinking witness of death and struggle –
accepted by fish, oyster and crab.

Let those heading for squalor and misery,
know that God is here, in all the workings –

He is the curtain of life that lives in waves;
that lives in wind and shifts the sand.

Bow Wave of the Yellow Submarine

It split like exhaustion in the shallows of my tea.

It suddenly hit me that all hope was gone.
It was years later – isolated by time –
that ticking thing – that ever-pushing-on.
It nudged me away from all I knew,
and the small things that came to set me true.
Things I thought were good and settled,
but youth is scarce now and birthdays blue.
They are more of a falling sensation,
where they once were relief –
a climbing to a higher light – a golden fleece.
Perhaps a chalice, or a Holy Grail –
maybe just the sunlight on a yellow sail –
maybe something special – a coloured submarine?
I remember that icon, with its joyful theme –
"We all live in a yellow submarine."

It developed into a mystical cloud – said out-loud,
somewhere between God and Krishna,
and numbered nine –
all according to the gospel of George –
a guitarist, who was in many ways divine.
It was a pseudo-religion that we never let go –
shunning wars and fears
with its sympathetic glow.
It was an optimism of hills and winding roads,
which I climbed in isolation – to achieve the aspect of a fool.

And looking down on Strawberry Fields,
my eyes were fogged by the musicality of tears –
for our submerged hull had sustained a crack
from all this ponderance of looking back.
It split like exhaustion in the shallows of my tea,
where my joy dissolved like sugar lumps...

    I let it be.

The sixties were a defining path –
undeniably loyal and good –
a magical bus through the neighbourhood.
It was as if the meaning of everything –
every solution and every tide –
was flowing in the existential vibe
of the common heart of Beatle blood.

I STILL FAIL

I have stepped into the cradle of simple intensions.

Unless you are reading this, I am a failure,
so for now, I will read it to myself.
I will read it bigger than it is,
like the start of something special –
the roots of God, or the arms of an octopus –
the beginning of an episode of The Outer Limits,
blaring its intentions with an American accent –
the full hitch, loud and condescending –
more like a newsreel than the structure of a poem.
Let it be a headline, thrown into the common street
to grind its blatant story to a desert dust.
Let it creep into the hollows of this empty house
till it runs out of breath below Victorian high windows.
A conclusion is resolved at my spiralling stairwell;
at the angled steps that whirl like spokes –
meandering demons, marking levels of darkness;
a parasitic plant – with a full stomach of poison.
It is waiting to dissolve the dissenting charm
of my mediocre thought and its patterned ways –
all tooled-up for a conforming lament;
a leap into a cloistered temptation of mystery.

Let my words be mysterious then –
like all the best words are.
Words that compensate for the loose-lipped multitudes,
who chew their words full of stolen accuracy,

and do not reveal truth to the art of pleasantry,
unless hiding deep, among a cult of strangers.

I became a stranger as soon as possible;
promoted by success in the world of art.
It felt better to collect triumph safely in my hands
than to squander its complicated, unsociable starch.
It stiffened the many sides that riches contrive,
beyond the mere meandering scent of gold –
or the scenery of dust from a worthless heart –
not quite cruel or intentionally cold.
It was a world that no one else could enter;
and which I plundered with the dignity of a pirate soul –
too often boarding the merchant-ship of my own charisma,
never believing that one so wrong, yet so blessed,
could ever fail.

No one entered this plentiful world,
though I left the door, always open.
I watched them scurry by
like critics with the kettle on –
running past the leper-gates of my eternal endurance –
I even developed a skin disease for authenticities sake.

I was a mess; I was too late –
and retaliated with an occasional fuss,

'I Still Fail' continues...

or a desperately waved flag of national hate –
or a sheet of paper poems, ruthlessly transcribed
from the blood and veins of my punished head –
now shot open, like a Kennedy.

No one likes a death scene – only everyone –
but the slathering hordes did not attend.

So here it is – I read it for you now –
and in your face – as hideous as leprosy.
If it means nothing, then turn away,
but I have seen beyond your curving eyes
and know they look back too often to be indifferent.
I have seen past those exploring eyes
and seek to disarm them with a dangerous kiss.
I have stepped into the cradle of simple intensions;
beyond the permitted limit of accurate lies.
I have seen further than your definitions
and know I can still wear uncertainty –
if only in disguise.

I am your friend now – I have told the same lies,
both in panic and in public
and in darker times – the darkening death days,
where the crows fly backwards –
and circle away on an errand of pity.

They bring back more grease paint for their noble wings
and for the ludicrous imaginings of our acted lives.

As a precaution, I have taught myself
to leave the door open,
but balanced on the links of a securing chain.

And the door will be open – even after my death,
for the chain is the eternal symbol of the slave.
I will be enslaved by death – to listen for your knocking.
And the door will be open – after my life.

Do not be afraid to enter my living room;
this old ghost needs your charitable breath.
A bridge built in order to speak the right words
and span their meaning in a perfect way;
to obtain a new address in the library of scandal;
to allow their livid hearts to pour out their designs.
And let them choose their own designs (each lit by a candle)
placing their order in the spaces of rest.
These will resonate a need for popular culture,
and where they will live forever – an endangered species.
They will be lost among gods and their spare planets,
and in-spite of themselves and regardless of failure.

MY THURSDAY SHOES

I step forth, asking my shoes for guidance.

If it is Tuesday, I must leave by the window –
and on any other day, except Thursday.
On Thursday, I can leave by the door.

Thursday is an official walking day;
a day offered to the world – a day offered back.
I step forth, asking my shoes for guidance.
"Everything will be alright," they say,
expectant of a joyful return – a welcome home –
a crossing of the dimming threshold
of evening light.

On any other day, I may also leave by rumour,
using my mind as shoes –
but never at night.

LOST LANDS

My father's bike is rusting in a pond.

My father cycled through these lands
that now seem unreal and full of fake.
Nowhere near as tidy as those honest days,
before workers were encouraged to stay at home –
employed by the government to eat cake.
I feel a draft chill my heart – and I will move on.
Our blood and history are not required –
our kind are gone.

My father's bike is rusting in a pond –
or displayed outside a shop of antiques?
Its brakes stiff and its tyres flat,
and all my father's peddling, resting beside it in a heap.
It is surplus without his spirit –
and so are the fruitful hours of progress
he peddled out – street by street.

My father has ridden further now – and gone to sleep.
When I saw him last, he was laying on a bed –
quite empty and fully dead, where over-burdened nurses
had left him quiet of dignity –
except for that peace he now assembled for himself –
with a suddenly bright and patient charisma.
They did not know that man, or the books he read;
they did not understand the gentleman
that thrived in every hair upon his head.

'Lost Lands' continues…

They talked of holidays in their chattering corridor,
scribbling details on illegible charts.
I tried to decipher what they said –
but they were just directions for the death cart.

I was in dread – there had been no time to say:
"Do not go gentle into this sullen day..."
He had left his head;
he had slipped away on a windblown thread
and gone off walking, like a child –
to find another bike – to find his roving legs –
to find another path to take him home.

It was a road he had travelled all his life,
almost orphaned, after his mother was gone.
She died in the epidemic after World War One.
At that time, death was everything –
my father was none.

His road was always a path back to her;
a journey through unrelenting lanes and ways.
Through rain and sun and our happier days –
those of birth and wedding bell... and on...
through darker times...
And now, on this last farewell,
and in the fullness of summer's blossoming lanes,

I imagine him glancing back, to wave a hand –
to wish all our future family well.

My father lived in a heaven of his own
and he did his best to guide our stars –
with a true energy of simple love
in the earthly presence of spirit and bone.

THE GHOST OF HOME

You and I were shepherd moons – for Judith

The privet hedge at Sellars Road,
grown from twigs, is still intact, I checked,
and my camera saw it too,
and even the colour had bled back,
from those black and white days,
where we had to smudge the air with crayons
to fire some colour.

I arrived again last June.
It was as bright a day as ever bloomed
and we were there – all of us, in our way –
all baked into those bricks of clay.
Or we were happy seaweed at the coast –
a waving tide of an immersive host.
With ripples heading out like radio waves
to test the world – to find the paths that suited most.

The tea-cup rooms survive too, no doubt,
but only as echoes now
behind someone else's other noise.
But it is still enough to allow a thought
to sit in any of those lost, familiar chairs.
Or on the edge of a quiet bed
in the comforting folds of upstairs.

Herbert's bike was never in the way,

and won't be now, even as a ghost.
And tea-time will still be celebrated
with little houses made of toast.
Betty will arrive in the afternoon
with her shopping bag and coloured pens.
And David, will remain aloof,
walking away with his gang of friends.
And June, our mysterious dancing girl,
will flit in and out, in a subtle whirl,
and Stephen will always be there –
sometimes even more than her.

(They sat together in the living room,
pretending to be married, until they finally were)

You and I were shepherd moons
orbiting everyone else's day.
Always interesting – with something to offer
and always something to ask, or say.
And even when the sky drew dark,
we kept that flame and lit the spark,
with our little worlds of toys and games –
our worlds apart were both the same.

AN EXAMINATION OF EXPLANATION

I taught my senses to learn from each other.

I know what is wrong with my head –
it thinks that I left my senses for another.
But she shone with the brightness
of that subtlety of soul
that is hard to resist on any side of level.
It now grieves with the guilt of a blackened heart,
and has issued due pain ever since.

I taught my senses to learn from each other,
as I learned guilt from all of them.
It was a classroom of hurt –
one lesson toppling another,
while I, in confusion, threw chalk at my head –
I was waking up from my wildest dreams;
I was drawing my attention to the front of class.

The art of writing it down does not matter –
only words favouring silence should be used,
for inside their kernel is our true measure –
languishing with our senses, battered and bruised.
Other ciphers lurk in the mood of clatter –
where we are ugly from stitching the anguished thread.
We scribble it out onto the page of deception –
our spider's pen – our wanting web.

THE URGE TO RAGE ON

Let us not lose the message of breath.

Let us speak out
before speaking is moored
to the delicate harbour
of nervous fools.

Let us speak from the heartache,
while the heart may still be expressed.

Let us sing the song of freedom,
while it remains a blесséd chant.

Let the blind, who live amongst secret doors,
reveal the passion of a searching soul.

We will be silenced for years
of falling words
if human rage
swallows its dose of death.

Let us not lose the message of breath
to the cancellers, and their emptiest babble.

I HAVE LIVED MYSELF ALL WRONG

I am a solitary man, without charts.

Some will think these last hours of my being are a curse,
but I see them in triumph – call my nurse.
I will need to rehearse this final fate
like it never happened –
or that it happen to someone else
and much too late.
Call me a scoundrel, I will look away,
while you bang your head against a popular wall.
I feel your dismay, but need no lesson of grief
from the bare cupboard of a livid mind.
I am a solitary man, without charts –
when I choose to leave, I will blow away.

Nor do I need your forensic eyes –
or their charming smile – or their vicious darts...
and certainly not those tipped with poison
and ruthlessly aimed to stop my start.
Throw me a paper dart of joy –
throw me a kite of pleasure,
I will fly it up to the highest shelf,
where my books found rest for their holy treasure.
(and where the latest season of gathered dust
betrays the age of a valid endeavour.)

Or I will bend it into the mystery of a spiral shell,
twisting the guideline through cell upon cell,

until I truly connect a wire to God,
where his infinite fabric bends to listen...
would God really listen to me?

Like hell.

So I am going anyway –
I have always been going some wretched day.
But first, I need to become someone else.

HIDING IN THE LONG GRASS

Something forbidden-looking... yet born.

i

The world churns its chaos and brings me poems.
They are warped in my background of unruly grass.
As though the issues of deceit from a fairground mirror
are as instantly mysterious as unfaithful love –
it is a 'corner of an eye' thing –
nothing seen or settled –
it is a natural curse I must unfold in a pentacle.

> *Unwrapping its black garments of exhausted fire;*
> *dousing their meaning with the flat of an iron;*
> *reversing the curling of wrought iron words*
> *and their infatuation with the orbit of wheels.*

These curved ways are hard at first –
too darkly-fancy for human ears.
And it is never enough to leave them hitched
to the weak suspension of their own anxieties.

ii

I feel like a fly stuck on glue paper –
hanging from a ceiling-light – not quite dead.
Some sort of Jesus fly, chosen to suffer
(death is every minute a saviour – none are exempt.)
There will always be room for the disciples of rapture –
and the receivers of poetic, god-like favour.

But my own companions seem makeshift now
with no easy tools to contact their hearts –
no perfect identity, that would tally with trust,
or with their own sharp countenance,
spanning years of conversation.

I will lay very still in the patterns of nature,
turning the pages of a fruitless day.
Lost in recordings of my camouflaged gossip –
that elemental wisdom of accepted dismay.

iii
From my new position in the long grass,
I have no way to force a fury from my plough –
to scatter the seeds of a brighter future –
a sunlit spot, in which to live – or how.

This world gives little pleasure now –

And even then, it is in the shadow of a loan:
paid back in the meagre abundance of equity –
or the gross instalments, torn from my wings –
stripped from my DNA's balding stub.
That frightening core of charming real-estate,
where death is responsible for stolen peace.
And there I lay, in mourning for my life;

'Hiding in the Long Grass' continues...

creased with breath – smeared with grease.
I had slipped off my roof and fallen into my lawn,
embedding myself in the history of gardening.
And there I have lain, laughing ever since,
as the grass grew long beneath a rumbling thunder.

It was a perfect lawn without my impression –
I rolled it with stripes under the charming Sun.
Now it grows far beyond health and reason –
it is wild and cunning – with an assortment of seeds.

These seeds are offered to the loose hands of the wind.
They harbour life and death in the folds of earth –
they are something stuck in the teeth of chaos;
lost in the rooting shadows of this modest tomb.

iv
Long grass hides everything, including me;
it hides my frequent visits to the sea –
for even as a fugitive sailor, I have travelled far –
a being, configured beyond all recognition,
to crawl across the open sands
and stretch my eyes with a windswept vision.
My blood and spirit leech out of wet stones –
those forming the colossus of a sea-bashed wall.
They drip from soiled pipes, that leak as one

and bleed from every crusted union.
My rust is an entertainment now –
a vile offering, inviting discretion –
it is a record of my treacherous bile,
yet still a paragon of tainted trust.

I will remain a representative of death's holiday,
and I am convinced that role has always been my call:
to bleed into a world that stirs up new poems,
and leaches them out to the minds of the world.

v

A glance is enough for a portrait to breathe –
and eventually, words return the favour of song.
And so am I – hidden in a renegade lawn –
frog-like now, but with perfect hands.

2
PART TWO

A Recommended Heart

AMBASSADORS OF TRAVEL AND PILLAGE

Yet it would not hurt to turn away.

Wide deserts, resting in centuries of shifting dust,
tempt roads to wind through them,
as snakes or scars.
Deserts are built that way – with wide emotions
and the serpent stare of hypnotic eyes.
They are mere illusion, for enchantment's sake.

These roads rattle out from the cool of night,
when the sun shakes the limits of compressed bones;
poking them with sticks of searing light.
You can hear them cracking –
these cleft-feet of stone –
and by noon, you feel their monumental ache.

Our restless limbs take us to our latest mistake –
that need to travel, on frivolous minds;
light with inadequate local knowledge –
aware of ritual, yet void of respect.
Our careless misdemeanour – a scant observance –
yet it would not hurt to turn away.

We tamper with the culture of foreign lands,
prising their grip in search of pearls –
that beauty, smoothed by oyster-hard centuries,
crafted in the gritted teeth of living sands.

I CAN HEAR THE SEA

It is down there doing its washing up.

I can hear the sea behind me, behind the other me,
the me in this hotel – the me now looking out to sea.
It is down there doing its washing up,
with broken teacup-shells and stones,
and with the churning thoughts of sooner days,
swirling amongst the whipped-up sand,
the colour of weak tea.

Later, I will go down to the foot of the hotel –
down in the cage that creaks like a lift –
that slides past every wanting floor
in defence of expediency and miracle.
And there is a window in every passing door
and a face at every passing window –
all witnessing the business of descent.

And there is always a carpet out to the street.
In fact, the carpet becomes a street –
running the wall to wall of predictable lives;
tumbling down the steps of noon – a falling tide.
It is a street I know, and I have stood in its waters,
well before I first crawled free –
free of this taunting sea.

Was I an adventurer? A swimmer? An infidel imposter?
Blind empathy and rumour will do the rest.

But the rest is gossip, overridden by fatigue,
and set apart from the duty of a last, exhaled breath.

Last night a wave knocked on my door;
it could be heard through the cushions of my sleep.
It left some seaweed on the balcony floor
and on the welcome mat, I leave outside.
I always look for evidence like that –
though you can't miss seaweed on a welcome mat.

It was a calling card, and still damp –
delivered to my part of this huge facade –
asking my heart, with its seductive reach
to take part in the dreadful, drowning deep.

I will go down to the sea and become driftwood.
I will linger at its edges, incomplete.
I will loiter, like the shell of a dead oyster;
like an annoying trespasser – imprisoned by his feet.
I will pout like a doubting professor,
relinquishing his best theories just to agree.
Or I will become someone else entirely –
a new and welcoming, washed-up-me.
I will be rooted in anonymity, yet free.

THE SEASIDERS

for Judith.

We travelled by coach or railway train,
or the padded luxury of an old aunty's car –
each of us hustled on the grip of wheels
and the stifling imposition of stiffening bones.
It was the arrival that mattered,
the routes were just clones – puzzling epics
through the local shires.

And there were more puzzles to keep us quiet –
games accompanied by the medicine of sweets.
These were administered from a mother's hand,
alleviating the surprise of intrinsic bends;
quelling the edgy, sea-incited riot –
an unrest that our compensating hearts unrolled –
and there were the splashing voices of a happy tide
and a seaside flag, soon unfurled.

Eventually, we would see the sea,
shimmering resplendent behind blurring trees.
Or way off, beyond the singing fields,
or a heavy crop of ripening greens.
It was the living sea, hiding its deeper toil
beneath a trusted hue –
with the sky's ministry, governing all emotions
in the reflecting waves of fluctuating blue.

Then we'd be in a cabin, or a caravan,
or a rented room with a meagre view...
and the presence of the sea, a few streets on,
would hush our thoughts of restless talk;
pushing my suddenly unseated mind
into a silence of unsolved melancholy.

I never knew why that song adhered;
that doubting song, heard long ago.
Murmuring – out beyond the edge of land,
where the beach slid down,
like a drowning child,
slipping its folds beneath leagues of nought –
and down and down, into the persecuting depths,
where the continental shelf gave way to depression,
and the darker waves of spontaneous regret.

THE LOOSE ENDS OF TWO LIVES

Only the knowing of a neutral cat.

Walking downhill from the Temple Hotel,
my car parked high, in the late evening damp –
it is deeply dark, and with winter coming on
there is no one out in the quiet – thank God.
Only the knowing of a neutral cat.

My shoes sound out the cobbled path,
down to the street where the river runs slow –
and where the deeper sea of a false promenade
holds a misted halo to every lamp.
They murmur and flicker in a saturating damp.

My keys are ready – the one and the other –
in the shared dark of a single pocket.
I am returning on the burden of devotional disgrace;
swaying from one cherished life
to another.

THE MIND HOUSE

I will have the mind of a house when I have gone.

Where will I go when my house is gone?
This ghost I am, will suffer centuries of cold.

Where will I go when my house is closed?
Where will this ghost go to haunt its mind?

I will have the mind of a house when I have gone,
with many new windows and secret doors.

They will be trimmed shut to void daylight,
but I will open every single one.

THE GHOST OF PETER PAN

I let myself in through a borrowed crack.

I fell through your window while you were sleeping
and looked to see what books you were dreaming.
They leant as sentries, resting on your shelves,
or supine, as dead kings on your bedside altar.
I looked to read the tea leaves in your cup,
searching for the shapes of modern days –
fascinated by the subtle brush, where your lips had been –
and where the kiss was made.

It was a hard night, I could tell –
one where dreams are wholly disturbed –
rolling as they do, over invented coals
that make no sense – even to you.

I looked into your eyes while your eyes were closed –
they told more fury than any engaging stare.
The face has a different countenance with muted eyes –
a certain expression that is fully complete –
the still surface of the oracle, without surprise.

These so-called windows of the soul – the eyes –
are not needed to plumb a personality's depths –
it is a study of assurance – comparable to astrology,
where stars chart their field, under subdued breath –
they blush the room with quiet anxiety;
and welcome the souls of torment or friendship.

I was never Peter Pan, but in the absence of rules,
I let myself in, through a borrowed crack.
It was a pane first broken by a freezing wind,
that let me see behind your unchartered walls –
the simple details in the ranging shadows,
created by the negative of a dead lamp.
I wanted to see the flat hand of your table,
with its resting books in ambient occlusion,
and all the other secret places,
that wrapped this night in scheduled grace –
(a room with its eyes shut is as giving as a face.)

The rest of your life remains a mystery – and must,
but the waking life is unimportant to me –
except for the books you read out of trust,
scanning each of them, with a full sense of duty –
washing their pages in the sediments of tea.

After a while – a long while,
I clung to the window's sliding frame.
I was a thousand feet above my imagination
and my unimportant name.
I looked down then, to a world's shared troubles,
where we had been together, with closed eyes...
and without the need of a mutual word,
or those deluded fragments of sympathetic lies.

HEROES NEED HEROES

The Day Before Pop Culture Ceased to Exist – for David.

Unfettered by need of music,
the dance that rain performs
spat into our cup of words,
as we ran for cover
in streets of charcoal –
smudged by a storm in the ageing day.

The gutter was our friend –
we watched the water sail away.
Our religion, more a secret state,
without need of faith and a refusal to pray.
It was a religion of music; a turning page,
an anxiety of softened, mental rage.
A reincarnation in our need of return –
to do the things we had not done,
perhaps undo a few we had –
to learn the things we did not learn –
un-speak a word or two we said.
To say them in the places
they were meant to be heard,
which we still visit, in reverent dread.

These places are trapped inside a clock's chime –
a curved glass porthole in half-mirrored light.
        They move with us,
as we pass through this afternoon of night.

These are gods, or the mansions of gods,
lit with that special – 'tea-time' light.
A known panorama we could almost hug,
a warmed-up word we could almost say –
the clock's hands being our north and south,
and time, that finger and its written groove,
ruthlessly pointing another way.

As the rain broke down into our cup of song,
we sailed the High Street in an ancient boat.
The record shops had almost gone,
but there were heroes amongst them, still afloat.
Still warming papered windows with starry-eyes,
as we two searching souls, tried our best –
to blow the music home –
to push the sails –
to fill them with heroic breath.

Our ship now flounders in a rougher sea –
that chaotic beauty
of a Black Star's death.

9th January 2016

LOVE AND DARKNESS IN TESTAMENT

Without your glance, there is no meaningful look.

Without your innocence in the presence of sunlight,
my eyes have nowhere to look.
Without your body in the landscaped darkness,
I would be fumbling the pages of a barren book.
Without your eyes, I would have nothing to show,
and without your listening,
my words have nowhere to go.

Yet shall I take a road's long burden
into a future, bleak and often uncertain?

If your stars ever dim, my sky will blacken.
My mood will slip back through the door of my heart.
And restless and lost in a malaise of oblivion,
I would close my curtains and fall apart.

A Recommended Heart

See to your own heart and your desires.

When anarchy begins to confuse the world,
the world's listeners become fearful liars.
Let the world burn – for it is destined to burn.
See to your own heart and your desires.

See to those about you, who truly care;
those who do not insist you stay, or cut your hair.
Those who let you walk away,
displaying a heart's recommendation,
yet minimal concern.

THE KING OF NOTHING

The Possibility of Treason.

One day in my living room
I saw my face on a twenty-pound note.
It was not the face of a remembered artist –
nor a writer, or an engineer,
or the rhetorical portrait of a great statesmen,
lining his image with pockets of gold.
Instead, my face had replaced
that of His Majesty The King –
presenting itself in the guise of a monarch.

Suddenly overwhelmed by the possibility of treason,
I hid the note in the folds of my darkest wallet –
where, according to the critic,
living in my youngest son,
its secret was safe for years to come.

Yes I thought – until the world is dead –
and I had at last become the King of Nothing,
which, in the current realm
between distant living rooms,
I am already crowned.

CHRISTMAS LIGHTS IN CROCHET

Resting on that sill, in the blue and grey – for Lara

We thought they would never illuminate a room,
except for the joy of a windowsill?
But they glowed like magic in the light of day –
and in that knitted structure made entirely of our hearts.
And even at night they found their light –
resting on that sill, in the blue and grey.
Their wool, as warm as talk of home –
where they nattered on and always will.

FISHING OUT A HOME

Yet they sang of lives of grief and duty.

We were four miles out from the fires of Christmas –
from the corny trappings of human tides –
an unearthly light to guide us in,
bossing the stars like a winking heart.
The waves pushed the boat like a busy crowd,
jostling home after a rainswept match;
the fish died slowly, in the pit of our hold;
all life zeroed from their airtight world.
Yet they sang of lives of grief and duty,
and the merciless hooks of human survival –
but there was nothing they could teach us
about spanning millennia;
they knew short-term motives
were misguided, at best.

Where we may be lucky, even thrice, has no matter –
give us the right to live beyond human means;
beyond our night of looking seaward and back,
across that march of God's heaving concourse.

I was never without the thought of turning,
or twisting my own hook out of my lip,
and swimming back –
O swimming back
into my yearning.

THE GHOST LAYER

A turning of pages.

I can hear sounds from across the world
overlaying our own layer of common dust;
or we overlay them in mutual trust.

I am in a dark house in the early hours;
they say that every house
has its own particular sounds.

This house has the sound of all its ages,
which I call the ghost-layer –
a turning of pages.

Is our sound to be the last little echo?
Are we to be destroyed by the whimper of egos?

I am unsure, and will wait a night to see;
I am unsure, but will listen for thee.

HE SAW GHOSTS

The True Purpose of Apparitions.

He saw ghosts, but they were ghosts of himself;
the men he could have been
had he walked down certain corridors,
opened particular curtains and closed certain doors;
or attended demanding meetings – buoyant,
and with a heap of spirit.

They are lost now, those unkempt minutes,
under the old hours of forgotten days –
ploughed back into the unsown soil of intention;
trampled by the weight of human words.
You can see the dog-eared edges of his pages.
        A fallen agenda –
settled into the ribs of a shallow grave.
They are exposed and rattled by wind, always.

In summers gone, he wiped blue skies
from a soft complexion, held in trust.
He looked forward into that alluring haze –
that missing detail, that might not matter.
He gazed through open, honest eyes
and swam, submerged in the tepid shallows –
his great ship, languishing at low tide,
in its lee of negative possibility.
The ropes and masts marked their time
with sundial lines and critical angles –

all drawn taut in the heat of midday.

It was easy then, in comfortable youth,
to look too far into a proposed adventure,
until it seemed reckless – beyond bother;
it seemed suddenly and overwhelmingly right
to skirt those windless, brittle days –
the straights, the ocean reefs,
the undiscovered ways.
And in the end, it grew too late to sail.

He sat in the darkroom of a reclusive mind,
developing images that never were –
that would always be, unfocussed, grey –
and on being remembered, were occasionally unkind.
And looking back with maps and charts,
he realised he had circumnavigated his life,
while also circumventing a personal phase –
using histrionic crisis, as an elemental device.
Only ghosts would tell his drama now,
and that, he came to believe,
is the true purpose of apparitions –
to struggle, trapped, in the turmoil of unrolled days;
lost souls, which he now finds impossible to dismiss,
having cursed and failed them.

NO BREATH TO BLOW ME HOME

I was too capricious to be the 'chosen one' – for Winifred.

O love, where did we fall;
was it me with my creative call?
Lured sideways out of town
to a city's pandora's pot,
that I opened far too wide
and could not shut –
could not get the lid to close
on a slow and spurious plot.

I was too capricious to be the 'chosen one',
but my sudden halo, invoked by fools,
had crowned me king of creative thought –
where their intentions, although no doubt good,
were more about themselves,
and their need of a saviour.

I wandered through those mesmerising days,
that ticked the time into a sinking mud.
I should have listened to our own rules
and our acknowledged ways –
they were at least inventions of genuine love.
They were the jurisdiction of recommended hearts
who knew by instinct they had found each other,
in the careful patrol of misleading life –
a battle defeated by our accepted presence.
We had grown our rules from rare seeds

and watered them with the finest grace –
and assured ourselves as a perfect pair,
though a blind concept to so many eyes –
for we had drawn our lines so broad and free
only our stars could chase them back.

Eventually, our listing tower,
lurched in a mood of vague confusion.
It wrapped itself in stems of thorns –
that offered no sanctity for our pure embrace.
And were those swathes of pointed wreaths
wrapped by me to keep us safe?

It seemed as though our miracle
had failed its faithful grace –
it had lost its key,
and could not twist inside its ruins
to send its message home.

These unkind vines of impossible need
were the dreams of an immature,
and lost young man,
who had tried his best with a failing plan
to push aside their binding ways –
working like a gardener, with imperfect tools;
walking on water, in the wrong direction.

Gardens can be such destructive fools –
they run amok with tendril and weed.
They build our path with trip-wire days,
leaving us pondering our fateful step –
which will be borrowed anyway,
from pandora's curse,
and elements of what we think we know.

I turned my back then – to the north wind,
to use its blast to return to your heart,
but my twisted roots had changed their station –
grown into a deeper chaos – and for certain –
they had no breath to blow me home.

3
No Road Home

What Strangers Know

A POLAROID PRINT

Defending the shallows of its happy crowd.

A colourful day – in the 1930s hotel –
a casual luxury, over-looking the sea –
I am a camera, and you are my subject –
most of my panorama –
almost one third of the scene.
I stare down the promenade to the working class harbour,
with its foaming edge, brushing milk to the deep –
pestering the sea wall, like the tyrant birds,
or smudging the fingerprints
of memories and dreams.
The rest of the tide and the sea beyond,
are held back by a curved arm of sand.
It seems almost a failing – a crippled machine,
defending the shallows of its happy crowd.

On this summer's day, the seaside is a shrine.
I focus on you, with blond, straightened hair –
with eyes of blue… or eyes of brown,
yet never standing in the way.
You are in the centre of the hunting frame,
where lens and eye,
focus the expanse of a grateful day.
The scene looks back like a Polaroid print,
announcing the glory of saturated colour.
It is now bestowed on people and things,
who came here to cure a mistrust of each other.

PHOTOGRAPHS FOR THE HISTORY CART

They are always looking for the doubtful glory.

In the 1930s, when photographs were eased from film,
Hitler was the most negative man in the world.
Using the tools of processing,
they cut into his image,
not looking for cancer or some visitation of evil –
or a ghoul, wedged inside a rotten heart –
they were looking for that persuasive charisma,
some would follow without doubt or question –
those finally crushed beneath the wheels
of the history cart.

They penetrated deep,
using confessional black and white,
while his image appeared as a spectral apparition –
slowly resolving in a devil's agitation:
developed in liquid beneath a safe red light.
It guarded the technicians' exposure to evils
they themselves, may not yet possess.
Though sometimes, it was they who summoned
fields of ghosts and whole backdrops of death.

Now the photographers swarm like worker bees,
as the SLRs – rattle on –
flapping at a pace beyond breathing hearts,
that now beats a persistence neath a digital sun –
and with reckless paparazzi souls watching on.

They are always looking for the doubtful glory,
or the useless, unforgiving thing.
Something to reflect itself in a prattling mirror,
or in the betraying whisper of a cell phone's eye.

These days, it can be anyone's turn... anyone's guess.
We are all the most photographed person in the world,
on certain days – at a given speech – a sporting success
or a meeting of minds –
where images are also occasionally unkind.
Or we could be victims of mayhem or terror,
whose heart of Hitler – black as death –
is still dissected in temples and books.

WHAT I WILL MISS, LIVING ON THE COAST

To Judith

What I will miss when living on the coast
is driving to the coast, listening to Leonard Cohen...
or David Byrne... or Wallace Stevens;
who talks about the idea of order at Key West.
I will miss stopping to question my sister,
who travelled there with me when we were young.
She now waits ahead, already seaward,
but will soon have to carry those last fathoms home.
We love each other, but know the measure of distance;
she loves the sea, but stands well back.

The sea air is a suddenly refreshing thing –
Byrne walks away with a wind in his face.
He polishes an eyeball in search of odd things;
following the promenade in its adagio of structure;
boarding a sea-shanty sung in his head.

Cohen and Stevens conduct a bare-knuckle fight,
there on the canvas of wind and sand.
They fish Ernest Hemingway out from the pebbles
and balance his jealousies into a biased referee.
He permits the use of solemn language,
and dry starfish as improvised weapons.
Cohen declines the advantage – while listening to the sea;
preferring to hear the rules, more distant than oppressive –
they are wrapped in the cunning organics of a shell

that mermaids have pressed to his paperback ear.
"The real sea is over," says Leonard to Stevens:
"now we must return to the energy of slaves."

The shell is a dry beast, still capable of living
and writes a column in the Daily Sand.
This week she will address the failings of Leonard,
who fights like a lover, with a graceful hand.

David Byrne returns with a small ice-scream,
removing his rhythms to relax in the foreground –
echoing the disorder in a musical sense,
as Wallace Stevens floors the cynical referee.
It was an accident, but people cheer him on,
feeling he has downed a significant bully.
Hemingway – no more than a bitter old man –
is killed by the blow and is washed out to sea.
He is pleased with the award of a literary surprise
and goes on to write about his death in the afternoon.

I will miss all that, when I no longer travel...
under the strained endeavours of elaborate confessions.
I will miss all that, when I am chained to a chair
in my seaside tomb, refusing to go out.

First published in 'Fevers of the Mind' – 2018

THE MIRRORED FACADE

We have studied the sea in terms of arrears.

I woke up in the top left-hand corner of a hotel.
At other times, I had woken in the middle –
above the letter 'O', or in other rooms,
advertised with balconies and various comforts.
Today though, it was the now favoured
top left-hand corner –
or top right-hand corner, as we faced the sea.
I with my dark and rusting bathyscaphe –
and you, with your beauty and the golden key.

The sea nudged the land with its creative ways,
full of destruction, as creativity is.
Showing us the secrets with its filtering lurch,
that washes this beach of broken bits.
Or what can be seen in the corner of an eye –
or from the corners of an antique hotel.

Last evening, at sundown, after the dinner bell,
its facade had closed like an iris to the night –
while one by one, each little light
turned its back in patient sleep.

We regard this hotel as a museum now;
one that in some ways represents our lives.
We have often come here to stand and stare –
glancing through the charmed windows

of heart and mind.
We come to study this most glorious exhibit –
the rolling tides of an ancient sea.
And at various times in all our visits,
we have studied the sea in terms of arrears –
a glancing back at our own spent lives,
trying for feelings that hold secure –
if not elsewhere, than at least here.

All these years of the sea are in evidence today,
and are stretching away from this glass facade.
Reaching back into its shards of time,
with their broken possibilities – both yours and mine.
And where inspiration once glued us together,
in a delinquent indulgence –
still favoured from time to time.

A TRIFLE

She had come to show me how to love you.

We went looking for your birthday cake –
a small one with disguised years –
more a token of persistent love,
which, throughout its time
has sometimes seemed a mistake.
Regardless, we rolled like the rolling tide –
in and out of our own favour.
But we survived long enough –
through the various clouds of our own behaviour.

We chose a chocolate cake as an emblem of desire.
It could have worn a candle and been stoked by fire,
but it bore the years in silence, without a flame –
without a light and without your name –
and all the nonsense illuminating fruitless questions
concerning age, or blame.

For these random excursions to the side of the sea,
at birthdays and invented times,
all carried the baggage of their burst balloon,
exhaling a white elephant into the room –
to mutter the unpacked, restless remains
of an unfinished marriage – with its candle-flames.

Then an angel of wisdom, shopping in our wake,
suggested we have a trifle too – not just cake.

She had seen our bargain-minded eyes and said:
"They're half-price – on the bottom shelf."
She also bought one for herself.
She was an angel, in the collision of our lives –
this coastal woman,
who could discern a pair of rolling waves –
especially those breaking on local shores.
They held the truth that none can hide,
and she knew we had merged on many beaches,
through many years and many ages,
and saw that our celebration
was of our special age of triumph –
an age that God had no numbers for;
a span deserving the enhancement of trifle,
if nothing more.

She had come to show me how to love you –
as I had loved and laughed with her before,
and what could be forgiven of a damaging guilt
in that constantly revolving door.

HIGH TIME AND TIDES

We were yearning for deliverance.

Walking along the promenade,
with the windblown sea climbing the stone wall,
and the railings of cut-out paper-dolls
driving us on with outstretched arms.

We were drenched by the next bilious wave
and cowered beneath the weight of it all.
Yet it pushed us on in defiant laughter,
towards the warm expanse of a distant hotel.

We were yearning for deliverance – to rid the sand,
from our salted clothes and their deepening pockets –
much deeper now, with twisting shells
and the random dark of contraband.

This poem was not published until many years later –
we should have drowned then and there,
in a brief encounter – "a tragic dalliance" –
exposed as a "trifle" in the evening paper.

WHAT STRANGERS KNOW

"I write for myself and for strangers." Gertrude Stein.

What strangers know that family only suspect,
or accept too effortlessly for the appreciation of grace,
so that its news grows quiet in the corner of a whisper;
in the wink of an eye, or an understated look.

What strangers know that families deny,
as an unanswered bell in the centre of a room –
that monolithic hell, cupped with rust and broken tone –
silent in the shadow of a dispiriting dome.

It houses a grievance of neglected sound –
that strangers know, yet families step around –
what it feels like to be understood by others;
to be welcome, amongst a band of brothers.

WOMAN AT THE WINDOW

As I would caress, if I too, owned the skill of shaping light.

On jigsaw days – you sit by the window,
finding pieces to click into place,
or "hammer home," as you like to say –
enacting blows and determination.
These are uncharacteristic of one so mild,
as you peck at these puzzles, more like a child –
a beautiful bird, with a feathered insistence,
fanning out a neat precision – and a distance.

And looking up, you look superb –
upholding grace, in whatever challenge.
Your hair is the blond you – that was black in 1982,
when we were hidden behind the pieces of a year;
unplaced in time – our part in the puzzle.

You have not aged either – age swept past your form
like it did not care – like wind-tunnel air,
finding the smoothest design to trace –
to move you through time with perfect grace.
I love to see your silhouette at the window.
I declare it has stopped me going insane –
the old glass, guiding light around your image,
and with a soft caress to show it cares –
as I would caress, if I too, owned the skill
of shaping light.

And in summer, often lightly dressed,
you are always photogenic, never fake –
in either colour or black and white
or a click by mistake.
The camera loves you, and will itself blush,
especially on those warm, relentless days,
that breathe through our room like a gorgeous wind,
turning the numbers of a ruthless clock;
peeling the special inventions of our ways.

There is laughter here and also doom,
but always something of you, in this jigsaw room.
We watch ourselves quicken, like a ripening crop,
and are always looking out for merciful rain.

I am a dark light, falling behind its own silhouette.
I see things with a natural regret –
like a piece of the puzzle that does not fit,
and will not hammer home... at least not yet.
I have shared a pleasant existence with you,
if one, sometimes called by anxieties name.
Yet in regard to your beauty's perfect repose:
if there is any piece missing, or does not fit at all,
it would be hard to explain.

SEALED LIPS

Some thoughts are for the past.

Some future pasts are better left unsaid.
So I am going to ignore the squeaking hinge
of your unoiled lips.
They will tell us anything we want to hear –
their only function is to transmit.
It need not be the truth either,
or may even be sanctioned by a devious brain.
We know that.

We also know we are partly insane,
and therefore not responsible
for what our lips might tell.
Sometimes lips are just an accessory
and reveal or hide the trusted tale –
including the telling rendezvous
with those rust-red gates of hell.

The mind has many corridors though,
in which to lose ourselves in slavish time.
I always stop somewhere along the line.
I suppose I could say – to gather my thoughts,
but some have slipped too far and gone astray.
And some of my better thoughts
have lost themselves in paranoid dreams,
where the fond memory of freedom of thinking,
refuses to exist, without ghetto or neighbourhood.

They exist only to haunt my brain –
and there are no passengers now, on this anxious train.
I ignored them far too long and far too well,
and they pretend to be dead when I collect their fare.
I hear their rattling tones in the baggage car –
        somewhere now haunted – and back in the day...
They want no funeral or eulogy read.
Some thoughts are for the past
and better left unsaid.

THE NIGHT HOUSE

Idling like an engine in a four-storey house.

I like to sit with no lights – in the early hours –
idling like an engine in a four-storey house.
It is only then, that the Victorian character
of this unvanquished building is again subdued –
breathing a glimmer of remembered years
into the village chill of its blackest river.
They exclude me, of course – this creature of night,
who hides his talent behind a need for shadows.
The night house is unaffected by daily lives –
our rituals, our modesties and our kitchen knives.
It is a stage – a theatre in the dark,
waiting for the next play to strike its spark –
to entertain these magical hours with written talk.
Its arrangement of props changes with time –
as waves do, and that wind through crops.
And there is always light from somewhere beyond
that guides its time and never stops.

With open curtains, I am entertained,
by a street lamp projecting flurries of snow.
It flickers its shadows amongst my gloom,
like demented moths on spooled film.
Or animated, haunting mists
that dissolve to ghosts – with little effect,
yet backed by the spooks of ambient light,
where morning stands a few miles off –

waiting for order in a mixed bag of rules.

And it will eat the gaping holes above windowsills;
eat them back from the unhinged night.
For now though, the house is quiet and polite.
Only the stair-light burns the silence –
its dripping chandelier, hanging like a sword –
threatened by the termination of a spent career.
It binds these four floors in a graduated toil
of descending depth and excavated dark;
it smooths the precious positive song
of a lost, descending lark.

The house is far from dormant though,
and passes its party from room to room –
translucent spirits dropping visiting cards
and ghostly smiles with brief applause –
remembering all the long-gone souls
who have climbed these stairs with human claws.
It has known Victorian chambers, the coal fires
and two world wars – and now it knows me.
And when I am gone, it will know where I was...
sitting in its darkness at half-past three.

NIGHT WORK

For I have felt an unheard dread.

It is an odd thing, morning,
when birds sing into my night.
I can hear them,
pulling down the light.
I will go to bed soon,
for I have felt an unheard dread,
snapping at my clock –
tapping at my head.
And I have heard the mice
retreat to shadow and shed;
or yawning in the corners
of my wainscotted walls.
I have heard that facsimile
of awakening souls –
when the first human obstacle
breaks the fragile night –
spilling the applecart
with insidious blight.

Being first born,
is a form of assault –
they crash into the world
with a thick, careless jolt.
The garbage truck
and brewery van –
all doing their worst,

as loud as they can.
And the sneak of traffic,
with its venomous hiss –
rises to a twilight,
where all peace is lost.

I will sleep till noon,
then wake depressed,
with negative thoughts,
not deserving of address.
But somehow,
I will be here at midnight,
where I will do my best.

I am a night person –
I haunt my stolen hours
and dispute the rest.

WAITING FOR YOU IN MY OWN LIGHT

A commendation of the dead and the dying.

Winifred has gone to witness an acceptance into church –
the body and spirit of an old acquaintance.

In the compression of evening,
it is grey inside your silent house –
all the colours running out of light
as they flatten out the old news,
like exhausted balloons,
no longer stretched tight,
to gag the going breath of day.
There is an autumn outside,
with a weary light,
and a subtle sun, well in cloud –
it stokes the ember-hearted leaves
where the gold still burns, quietly true.
It is a pause – out-loud,
with a small wind blowing through –
whispering last rites
to these glorious, amber hearts.
It is a sigh, and nothing more –
and not attached to cause or law.
It is an urge to coax the leaves to fall;
to offer rest within a map of friends.
They are strewn in death
with autumn breath –
asleep at half past five.

The clouds are a mettled voice of grey,
that talk their way past your wooden fence,
rolling off in a mumbling depth,
that thickens towards a winter shroud.
    They are leaving –
before the season becomes too loud;
before it lashes down our moving parts,
and everything that keeps us proud –
maintaining all and everything,
and the glowing engine of our simple streets.
These streets at least, have an autumn mood,
and are exhausted with their rusting life –
now swept aside or descending down,
amid this devout lament for industrial days.

O my friend of friends, please hurry home
from your mission of mercy and farewell,
before I and this moment and this noble town,
lean too far out and fall into Hell.

EVER-CLOSER STATIONS: A LAMENT

God knows we stepped outside our lives to try.

We are lost, you and I, in the deep seats of our lives –
pinned back and helpless,
as time rushes through our ever-closer stations.
It is time measured by design and desire,
and in the shortening tracks of a limited future –
cast in whims that briefly register
on the harassed pile of today's schedule.
Thus we ingratiate our whitewashed lives
with the implications of a reconcilable past.
There is a discipline of waiting too –
an eternity of wanting things to be right –
but also blessed and true,
in that casual blur of distracted longing.

Our steps march in calendar strides –
and in the cascading tickets of diminishing days.
Each measured fall, a gathering of leaves,
that builds into the frailty of whispered corners.
Proof gathers in these angular moments,
and is woven into the caressing stock
of our rooted years.

We turn to our children then and trust them not to fail.
As we mostly failed, except for them.
They shine in the lamp of our extended pride
and in the anxious stare of a caring ambition.

They are exemplary beings – beacons of light –
the illumination of our day and night.
Shining through the tunnel of our darkest cares
and brimming in the clouds of unconditional love.

A steam train rattled our stations once
with a splashing entourage of rainy days,
each one costing a remounted sun,
with its golden tax and indifferent haze –
all paced-out in blue-sky miles
that travelled on wind to somewhere bland.

Our portraits curled from their fixed corners,
and our corners withered into dog-eared weeks.
Yet we hung on – clinging to the vital storm –
to every detail of our gusting sermon.
All the litigations – and social tribunals,
listed in the challenge of our children's advance –

we willed them on –

resurrecting our ovations –
those lamented, in the remembered surge –
We willed them to prevail, as a sorcerer might –
using a deft hand or a well-timed veil.
It was our personal testament of youth and age,

and valid as a comment on looming failure.
Yet they had already conquered so much by then,
even the true difficulties of shoelace and romance.
They had mastered liberation and dangerous travel –
out into a universe and swinging back –
these brave comets of our own creation,
playing out a dalliance with an awkward star.

Those formative days are diminishing, or gone.
We wait for news in a fractured time –
a decaying age we might call the future,
were it not bound in reticence, and so tightly spun.
It is an age of past and present only –
an era of rumour and telephone calls
and the passage of silence that lasts too long,
in those early hours when we are alone.
We linger with imagination's thread,
that might yet frame their return to our lives –
those welcome silhouettes at the end of the path –
a blossom's portent of a wider summer –
the crowning glory of our friendly gate,
suddenly opened by a child's hand.

The blooming arch is a welcoming wreath
and so are the skylarks we imagine overhead.
And we are over-grown with posies and laurels –

the awards and achievements of long-term sacrifice.
In truth though, our offspring are glorified elsewhere –
in the kitchen arms of other lives.

They are still young enough to find the time,
to achieve the things we missed, or left behind.
But will they receive that calling – that urgent storm,
as we did, when muddled and broken, and far too late?
The urge of everything we never did – to wipe the slate?
God knows we stepped outside our lives to try.

They already seem weary of that pursuing fate,
or have not yet encountered the meaning of bliss.
Too readily convinced that love alone will suffice
and that love alone is the only anointing kiss.
It is as though marriage and family
are the only challenge left –
the sole ribbon worth breaking through
in the hundred-yards dash to death.
I swear I see them ageing in that joyous breath.
I see their outlines swaying, in unsteady silhouettes.

In the rain-painted heart of my colourful days,
I sometimes think it is still our call
to find those other – 'fallen by the wayside' ways –
those moments – left to us – to anoint with forgotten art,

still sounding-out their thundering abyss.
Our time was different –
its sense of achievement never quite stated –
more perilous, like the mood of grief.
And we had the division of awkward music,
with our own rebellion on extended play.
But there is little time for pointless musing,
and less-so for the things we left detached.
Yet it still seems there is something to voice,
and that is why I am here today –
reconciling love at the end of a poem.

We are lost in the deep seats of our splintered lives –
pinned back and helpless with tiny details,
as time rushes through our ever-closer stations –
with an affinity to ageing, we are foolish to deny.
And with aching bones it is hard to kneel –
and certainly it is hard to pray –
hard to say any words in contradiction
of something, still imagined – still reckless –
and perfect anyway.

4
NO ROAD HOME

The Sea Takes Me Home

TALES FROM THE TOWER OF BABEL

It is a language, not content to unite our minutes.

It is a language, not content to unite our minutes.

I have spanned the distance between you and me,
with the kind of thoughts that held us together
when we were truly friends, and free –
when we were rhyming words
in an invented language that only we knew...
until something slid between us – I am not sure who.
Some malevolent force that fell, pitiless,
from the void... from the blue.

This scourge did not know our detailed ways,
it was inverted and possessive, and poisoned our trail –
and there was always something dead upstream –
with poison fingerprints, rumoured in braille.
We were lost then – from the world,
but also from each other's sight.
The poison was something like a wave, or a fog –
one that swims inland – moving like a blight.
It was a relentless force –
that we tried, with inadequate tools, to warn away –
or find the bleaching spell to utter,
that would commit to cleansing the shape
of treachery.

It is a struggle for hands that may never meet again,

'The Tower Of Babel' continues...

to shake or hold, as in the days of casual discipline.
When you were the song of all my reasons,
and we were never deaf to the beauty of choirs.
But these poisonous maladies are the work of others –
marshmallow thugs with soft, round edges.
You fell into their arms like needed cushions,
and the subtleties of comfort
that we had nurtured without prejudice.

They became something far below relevance or regard –
diluted like teabags in a stronger brew.
The subliminal knowing of our righteous quest,
with all that learning, and its roads to freedom;
with all those charts of civil unrest.
They have been refolded now into a road not taken,
and have made all the difference to our wounded love.

I have lit a church of candles – as our saviour would.
It stretches out into the space of all our failings –
a path to follow with the light of God
that burns with the music of remembered humility.
It is a gesture I learnt from 'She of Devotion',
who lit her candles for everyone's concerns –
until the world was so pure and absolute and bright,
none could escape their gravity of love.
But candles are wax and we are so slight –

and without the holy grace of grateful peace
they will burn into the offerings of folded night.
There are times when I feel the curtain is closed
and I will never see your smile again.
I remember our last goodbye though –
with its solemn respect of mutual men.
We had gone back to burn some old brushwood
on the glorious fields of our living past;
to stoke an autumn fire from the embers of truth,
and the fruitful season of our hearts' council.
And with the good humour, that purified our air –
and always patrolled our mental stage –
feeding from the anecdotes of a pleasant age.

We are new men now – but not much different –
except for life's contents and its unwritten prose –
you, the younger, becoming older than me;
flowing over time, like a tap left on –
or said like words that will bleed you dry
in the babbling tower, where nothing rhymes.
It is a language, not content to unite our minutes,
and speaks in that special range of voice and tone,
where fate has cast our bitter limits,
in a foreign language – in a foreign zone,
and like all that is foreign, my voice is mistrusted,
when heard in the context of a broken home.

TALKING TO YOURSELVES

Through the back of your existence.

Eventually, having lived with a person far too long,
there is a sense that you cannot talk anymore
and be sure they are listening.
They have a way of looking at something else –
through the back of your existence –
listening elsewhere,
beyond the current trend of your lips.

You have become an entertainment by proxy;
and they have heard everything you have to say,
and for that matter – and for the time being –
so have you – with your bored heart.

Neither are listening to yourselves, or each other –
you are both pre-occupied in scheduled clutter;
a profound subsistence – weighing less than nothing;
both becoming quiet in an expanding zero.

Soon, you will meet again, as perfect strangers.
Your paths will cross, near the garden window,
or at the shared kitchen table
with a vase of Hydrangeas –
and you will begin talking again,
using brand new words –
and inexplicably fall into the pity of love.

I Am Not a Caring Soul

O comment, thou are not required from the unkind.

1

I am not a caring soul. I stopped caring in 1987.
I realised my emotions were hanging out like entrails –
an easy target for torturers and charities.
I was a piano keyboard with the lid left open –
stabbed at by anyone passing my life.

I am a suit now, when not in use.
I hang in a wardrobe that smells of dead days.
I am partly hiding, partly blind,
yet nonetheless comfortable in a conceptual shade.

My dark glasses rest in the root of my pocket,
having eclipsed the patrol of my luminous ideas –
certainly those thoughts about where to stand –
even stepping back behind these famous shirts.
It is true they are only good for a playboy beach,
or anywhere south, in the nineteen-eighties,
but they provide excellent cover,
and no one will disturb them –
not old shirts that are impeccably dead.
They are as dry as tobacco leaves from an old cigar –
too mean and stale to bring pleasure to this concept.

I also have a hairstyle you cannot measure,
or even discuss with the clarity of a comb.

'I Am Not a Caring Soul' continues...

It lingers on in a phase of uncertainty.
Not even sure of the time of day.

The etiquette of physics avoids my hair.
It is neither long, short, nor ostentatious –
but it idles now in a quiet languor –
and probably with a layer of Heisenberg's dust.
My hair is dyed, but not coloured –
merely another volume of hidden grey.
It threatens to make me look distinguished –
or at least forgotten, or careless of opinion…
Yes, forgotten… but would I have it that way?

Even here, in this old wardrobe
I hide my soul from complete erasure –
I am writing like an old scribe in fear of new light.
Still bathing in the book that first betrayed me,
when the establishment opened its crooked eyes.
They discussed my work – the part they liked –
the part their flippancy could not quite ignore;
the part that excited their churned up letters,
and made words that formed their witches' pot.

This has become the work that (above all else written)
the scribe now cherishes as his final legacy.
It is the hype of a type of 'greatest hits' –

a 'selected poems' and nothing more.
A chart announced by the sensibility of others,
who say, while speaking through golden teeth:

"I like this – it rolls well off the end of a cigarette;
it is a place of smoke, mirrors, and final regret.
It is a place I need not visit to forget –
or not quite yet, in the sludge of thinking."

Yet true comment serves only to tamper
with my own disintegrating and fruitless mind.
O comment, thou are not required from the unkind.

2
I can hear their army breathing –
marching beyond my closet door.
They have managed to rent out this entire floor
and even the room I failed to hide in.

TO DIE YOUNG

But with a jacket on and my hair combed

I wish I had known the courage to die young;
to have left the world at half-term,
before the future came, with insidious doubt,
now my body is in such a state I can barely get about.
Or is it my schedule that sees me running late?
Is it my mind heralding a fearful fate?
It had its first excursion somewhere in your heart,
back when we were young and divine –
pushing eighteen – in 1969
when the world set us easy enormities to do.

Now I am fearful of everything,
especially these streets of stew.

But with a jacket on and my hair combed,
I could still sneak out and find some truth –
something to make for better sleep,
beneath a less begrudging roof.
A martini perhaps at a midnight bar –
that might do?

Life is painful these days – life aches –
it flounders on its own mistakes,
offered as familiar grumbles, or a loaf of bread,
sliced to measure out the week.

My days are presented in sections now –
each beginning and ending as toast.

I could conceal myself in the guise of a sandwich;
hide in the slit of a French baguette?
Make my escape by lunchtime, at the latest,
leaving as something happy – without regret:
a ham salad with cheese, or a bread cigarette?
It would be my final attempt to appear normal –
in the form of something desirable and complete.
A paper bag to keep me disposable –
a final effort to fit into the street.
All is waste and food now
and shops are set like rows of teeth.

The green space that was a city's heart
is a blur, surrounded by a coloured slag –
the wreckage from these, our plastic days
of trays and upset apple-carts.
I will remain authentic to the end –
another half-eaten, rejected thought –
left on a bench in an empty park.

I wish I had known the courage to die young,
before the days grew sliced and dark.

HOME IS NOT WHERE THE FACE LIVES

My voice protests against its frowning disgrace.

This is my face – the place where I live, according to time.
But I know not where I live, and hate my face –
my voice protests against its frowning disgrace.
After all the grief it bestowed, it demands a kindness,
but I would rather be homeless than living here,
behind a mask of the Facebook human race –
and on saying that, I hate my voice.

THE SEA TAKES ME HOME

To a mysterious place, the wind knew –

When I died, the sea came inland –
an irregular tide,
looking for my house.
It rolled its waves onto my step –
licking them away like a pack of hounds;
smoothing my house
into a burial of sand.

And later, when the sea withdrew,
it took my dried-up heart and bones
to a mysterious place –
only the wind knew.
And where my borrowed water
lives again,
tumbling with the rhythms of breaking waves;
sorting an eternity of anonymous stones;
mixing the experience of all our cells
into a singular shell
where the wind moans.

BIRTHDAY BLUES IN HD

for David and John

I spent the last hours of my latest year
watching the wedding films,
where I had hunted the falling moments
with a passionate lens –
cutting seconds into circles of revolving love,
to mesh our lives in celebration.
They joined together, hand in glove,
passing their smiles to each other's faces –
one frame founding each ovation.

These films are records of pleasant days,
locked in their own beguiling minutes,
with faces alive, or sometimes dead –
but nothing is lost of a valid existence –
these friends can still be heard – and said.

You may think these films are past-records now,
of long gone days, folding back in time,
but they are everything to me –
they are ancient hieroglyphs in full HD –
I study them to learn what my future is about;
always surprised it is also about me.
They are a record of my boys, deciding their way;
my long-lost sons – who carry me to the future.
who carry me to the wait and see.
Meanwhile, I will continue to film the waves.

I have never been far wrong with the beach.
The sea is always ready to roll,
with its clockwork tides and its time and tension.
It tells the whole history of intrinsic invention,
but from much further back in time.

I can feel the waves turning now, for me –
arms outstretched and automatic;
or rippling out those special moments
that we dare not look to see –
that we will not allow to become pathetic:
like the presentation of broken shells,
and the many parts of dissected crabs,
and the etched shapes of ancient seaweed,

drawing unread runes around my feet.
Nobody wants me in my birthday blues,
and I would never film me – standing here –
amongst this wreckage of entropic stars,
watching the cosmos curl away –
tightening its spring of mortal coils.
They repeat their doom but will not let go
of the devil, loose beneath the skin –
beneath this same old sea – this constant wave
that each and every ward-of-love must be.

THE GRAIN OF HOPE

I can no longer thresh the balance of this brain's hay.

When our sons move away
to light new worlds with their stars,
there is no shine in the hours and minutes
they leave behind.
There is a thought to raise hope
from once abandoned work,
but my ambition is quiet – and my bones hurt.
I can no longer thresh the balance of this brain's hay,
into helpful bails – not cleanly, anyway –
not without leaving a grain intact
to wallow in that moment of haunting forgiveness.

This over-looked seed has closed its fist
amongst the windblown stalks of rolling fields.
Or lost its way in the solemn depths
of honey-coloured, haunted stacks –
where bail upon bail, is the harbour that hides them –
these unsown seeds of clenched ideas –
these fugitives – now under dormant rule,
beneath the camouflage of remembered skies.

Rain has no value here,
except to shape a terrain's disguise.

I still walk in the places we have lived,
but my step is less crucial without their call –

without their persistent questions,
       or their rescued fall.
But each man must follow his unique road
and ours have forked their different ways.
My road is a narrowing lane of lost decades,
scattered by distraction and suffocating delays.
I will build a bridge with the steps not taken –
back to the grail of a calling vocation.
Its eternal children of art and words,
will bear the flag of unforgivable glory.

BROKEN HOME

Never being the perfect recluse.

I cannot wait to hurry home,
but make straight for the window
and look outside;
never being the perfect recluse
or adequate host.

I have long betrayed
the order of both,
and live inside a silence now
with a rebelling shame.

In truth, I have a yearning heart
to resurrect the joy I might reclaim –
restore the life I lost in moods
of depression, guilt and blame.

ESCAPE VELOCITY

Seven miles per second – and make it last.

I was hoping to escape the gravity of Earth,
but I would have to travel incredibly fast –
seven miles per second – and make it last.

That is twenty-five thousand miles per hour,
which I admit, used to be my favourite speed,
but not now – my brakes are binding
and my traction is in need.

I was hoping to escape the gravity of living;
to take it easy in a weightless hush –
a quiet orbit – high and wide –
and beyond the snarl of the daily rush.

I LIKE BEING IN MY CAR

There is no end to unchartered roads.

Driving between here and where,
there are no riches greater than stars.
There is no end to unchartered roads.
There is no enchantment I can bear,
without the endless moving on.

An endless dawn – an endless night,
always rests within my heart.
When I am driving back to you and you,
yet never going home.

DIRT ROAD

I feel like an old car abandoned on a dirt road
with grass growing through my heart.
Parked some years ago,
where the shrinking tank of hope ran dry
and my engine lungs gave out –
gasping a last, exhausted sigh.
The wind continued down the road,
with my unrolled maps and my smiling destinations;
they emerged like traitors through a steaming grill
and the rigid countenance of my headlight stare.
It was a refusing wind, as some winds are...
no longer passing my shape along the ways;
no longer brushing back my carefree hair.
And there is certainly no road to the future from here,
only the speeding grass hiding my zeroed dials –
and the almost perfect hours when nothing smiles
and birds sing my headlights to sleep.

THE FRUITS OF AUTUMN

An uncommon eye of understanding

1

And we, as leaves on the broken bough,
where the fruits of autumn
sweetened our last decades,
laughed best on the bridal path,
or the high fields where the horses ran.

We knew ourselves from a unique perspective,
that no others could, or can conceive –
an uncommon eye of understanding,
with a perfect depth of mutual-belief.
We cast up our errors for the microscope,
yet made them small and incomplete –
almost intended – a playful deceit.

These ripples of the heart were always overwhelmed
by the unwavering footprints of our synchronised steps.
Ours was a footpath, of many stiles,
with waist-high wheat and simmering regret –
          still picking blackberries in panoramic heat –
and always travelling with an engine of love.

2
After a while, the fruits of autumn
become dry sticks – unholy and forgotten.
Colours, once embers, are suddenly ash,

stained and bloodless,
without the animation of bones.

Or as leaves, rippling on a broken bough
might turn against a cooler breeze,
or fall into sleep on rumours of winter –
and rest into earth, on the chill voice of death.
Not us though, not now –
we will linger forever in these summer fields,
with the flight of fairies and the energy of sprite.
We sweetened our years
with the fruits of autumn – picking each other –
for a love, still-ripe.

I WILL CALL AGAIN

To the immersive peace of the dove.

I wish I was sitting, this afternoon,
in the front room of your warmth and love.
As yesterday fades, into a comfort of time –
there by my coffee, my biscuit, my set-aside gloves –
settled as I was – and still in love.

As close as I will ever be
to the immersive peace of the dove.

I am at my best near your heart,
when I am totally disarmed
and looking for nothing –
not even for the why we fell – not quite apart.
And not like the hawk I am today –
not like this cynical bird of prey.

I prefer to perch at the window of your world,
where the garden looks like a huge bouquet.
And I like to watch the tiring sun
frame the bright borders of your simple lawn,
then slide its patterns down trees and pears
to rejoice in the heaven of evensong.
We are all involved in a sleepy anon –
and the Robin on the bird-table,
suspicious of a breeze –
is soon disturbed and quickly gone.

And beware the dismissive cat you hate,
melting into the undergrowth by the arched gate.

Each movement is a tick of the clock,
and our time together is running late.
We bury that negative procession with talk,
and when there's nothing much to say,
we write on the air using secret chalk.
There is never silence –
like there is never silence for the rising lark,
singing its way to a welcome heaven.

And there is never anything we would not want,
and nothing we would ever doubt...
and even when we are both gone,
I will call again, through the wired cosmos,
and never find you out.

SHADOWS IN SHARED PLACES

And the times we could have focused the Sun.

Most days now, when I come to call,
we visit the walled garden,
with its ancient instrument –
a sundial – capable of teasing our light –
angling time out of the sun's slow shadows.
Everything is focussed on this one concern,
where plants tangle into their knotted days –
with light and shade pushing their tendrils,
and the energy of flowers,
unfolding the shade.

On sunless days, the world swings in –
using Earth's broader pendulum of light and dark,
and all its subtle shafts of doubt and spark
that arc their mobility into ripened juices.
I can feel my blood – stored in the sunlight –
shadowing our next awaited talk,
when we will speak of our children
and of our children's children,
and of our own roots and future branches.
And of course, the various houses –
and the times we could have focussed the Sun –
if we had cast more shadows
into shared places.

5
NO ROAD HOME
Late in the Day

A LOOKING-GLASS POND

And I cannot agree with myself anymore.

I have failed in my heart to find a way to live.
I almost live the way I please,
but my heart cannot find it right, or good.
My heart and my mind have disconnected –
they have turned the dial to misunderstood.
My room is a pond and they float on its surface,
drifting apart – I would say, on purpose.
They hate each other,
and I cannot agree with this self anymore.
There are bullrushes in the corner
and water lilies near the door.
They remind me of Monet – an old man of rainbows,
treading on softness in a repeated life –
smudging the detail with a blind inquisition.

I am almost blind myself, but in a different way.
I have chosen not to follow my path of resistance.
I have tripped over my own baggage once too often
but I am always packed and ready to leave.
I still read a little to pass the days
and fear the clichéd images of vast television.
They make fools of men and their simple ways,
and broadcast imprecisely, like malicious demons.
Everything is a cartoon, drawn from insanity –
and even the newsreader is a gameshow host.
There are certainly things they cannot tell us –

'A Looking-Glass Pond' continues...

and there are scheduled times for the things they sell us.
They hide the rest, like underwear in a drawer,
where a presenter's smile carries a whiff of evil.
I have heard the rumours of their secret closet;
it is locked, but ransacked by propaganda –
all hidden behind a fascist fascia –
that polished facade we cannot live with.

I too was polished once – potentially brilliant.
I shone with ideas and felt resilient,
but my ideas wept into the lead of truth –
it was embedded in their soul and weighed them down –
a base metal that would not become gold,
yet melted easily into a heavy frown.
In order to express myself I have become an alloy –
a tin man, mixed with the me of a softer self –
too malleable to be trusted, but at the first sign of caution,
I whisper a warning inside every bell.

I dragged myself down – a dull boy – partly drowned –
having lost his purity to the wonders of alchemy,
where even death refuses to say his name –
as I do now, in conflict with time and person –
a golden fish inside a steady bowl –
an honest leper, shunned for the stigma
of not getting better.

I behave like a collector of past and present,
with firm rules concerning future days;
and will not accept unfinished consequences,
the folly of fools – or the unopened letter –
those bags of silence, filled with rumour.

I am tired of living and tired of death.
I am tired of everything in between.
Let me go now, I have done your bidding.
Let me go to Little Gidding.

(This journey has already cost
not less than everything.*)

Let me be consumed by fire
and saved from your stage of endless mire.
I attempted life in your diary of pages,
but seal that treacherous book
beneath a rock of ages –
I will gladly press my palm into the cover
and swear it true.

LATE IN THE DAY

And this is the city that betrayed its nation.

As sunset ships slide through the shadows
and sail across the walls of evening.
And the clock ticks hollow on the languid mantel,
as the past and present define themselves.
They home and flounder on this vulnerable shore
with their constellations of cosmic stars,
snagged in the reflections of picture frames,
or creeping with the minute hand –
exploring the vase.

It is the light of apple dust – sprinkled in air,
while promising the earth and sometimes more –
the golden fruits and chaliced drinks,
all from a commerce of essential greed,

(that in playing our part,
we choose to ignore)

as we ignore the signals of a fallen city,
these – the diminishing roots of home.

Its mountainous flags of skyless buildings
drown the monuments of forgotten kings.
Its teaming river, throwing back waste,
full of the none-cosmopolitan, simple things.
And the ever-sliding door of wanting despair

that channels the lust of modern slavers.
They live off a land with a careless door,
that pampers the rich, and virtuous charity.

And this is the city that betrayed its nation
with pretentious art and dubious links.
And this is London, in the sunset hour.
Once made desirable by the Kinks.

PULSATING CITY

Your reflections are spectacular, but are a trap.

I will not come down to your water's edge.
Your reflections are spectacular, but are a trap.
I have known traps before and I know yours now,
or at least I know your tempting bait.
I see beyond the hook.
I see your total anarchy, snapping at its gate –
talking with a vicious lip,
about soldiers from the soul –
those who have only peace to proffer
in the blind alleys of ceded control.
Your wet hem seeps the ugliness of vice,
into the lowest regions of your highest towers.
The next time London smiles of folly,
she will not be ours.

A Forgotten Narrator

Those lost and interrupted souls.

Does anyone actually live here –
in the care home?
In the don't come home?

It is labelled to instil
the inspiration of confidence
into all its patrons,
and their sunniest days.

Where wheelchair grease,
is smeared like ointment
amongst silent relatives
and their clock of caring –

those baffled souls,
conscripted into a confusion –
of jigsaw memories
and misplaced mystery;

It is an intertwining with theirs and others,
represented here as stubborn snakes.
Where the Sword of Damocles
replaces the Caduceus –
a suspended drama
of their death
at night.

THE EVENTUAL SOULS

The fools of woke think revenge is justice.

The fools of woke think revenge is justice;
but only old souls can pass this way.
Only they have seen the renegade future.
Only they will fight to save a culture,
that fools regard as a blight on history,
and seem intent on giving away.
They think damnation is a cult of credit,
where their gang of friends comes back their way,
but eventual-souls are an entanglement of spirit,
writhing in a wind of endless change.
It is a natural force that meets no courage
and is not required to blow straight again.

A GOOD DAY TO DIE?

I knew I was deceased when I read my obituary.

I knew I was deceased when I read my obituary.
Not because I had been mistakenly listed
amongst the dead,
but because they had nothing good to say
about my conduct or my caring nature,
when all my life I have striven to attain
a respectable level of *reasonably okay*.
And it is hard to seem more blatantly relic
than a headline announcing:
"Shot by the Police while running away."

At least their elegy, so to speak,
was written in the brief, inconsolable tones
of agreed dismay.

THE WENTWORTH PILGRIMS

We had left the evening in their care.

The old men are going now.
They have waved enough in recent years
for it to seem polite to slip away
without a final word.
To leave the last of them
to tell us who they were, and why.
To surprise us with a final detail, yet unheard.
A revelation, saved to say goodbye.

The ageless stones will list their names –
as these pilgrim men had listed all before,
and enlightened us to a forgotten age,
or a story told again – once more.
It is now a posthumous chime,
that the bells sing in the high church tower.
It was their personal tour of pilgrimage and lore,
to this, their own remembered hour.

The ageless stones will list their names –
as these worthy men had listed those before,
and enlightened us to a forgotten age,
engraved across a graveyard floor.
With quiet companions, knowingly doomed,
they walked their days as flowers bloomed
and hedgerows frowned in Autumn's gown,
as it darkened on our road to town.

We had left the evening in their care –
these godly men, who had said farewell,
and we thanked the sunlit, blesséd hours
that woke their souls and brought them there.

LATE IN THE EVENING WHEN I HAVE GONE

And when I am just a waft of air.

Do not let my poems die with me.
Let them live in your secret moments,
side by side with your hope, or anxiety –
a little more dust on the mantlepiece?

And although I may seem to need to die,
my poems have always sought a life –
an inquiry into its little truths
that add together and oppose the lie.

And when I am just a waft of air,
that fabled bird on a thinning wire –
remember my poems chose to buy a house,
to draw the shades and light a fire.

THE FLICKBOOK OF THE PAST

Placing age upon remembered age.

As I walk away from Winifred's house,
down the long drive to a restless car,
I feel the book-of-the-past flicking animated days,
out from the pages of a pondering mind.
There are words and feelings and lost ambitions –
unsaid things, without need of saying –
all scribbled in the corners of these flickbook pages
that stutter with motion in an ancient air.
They move unfettered – their arms and legs,
dancing their way through remembered times.
They are flickering memories and pleasant rhymes,
painting old scenes of sun and children;
of barbecues and music – and washing lines.
These waved flags of various fashions,
are the iconic clothes of clockwork minds.
And there are familiar plants, grown from seed or twig –
and the apple tree that grew too big.

These things adorned a changing stage –
placing age upon remembered age.
And heard in the laughter of beloved sons –
from babies to teenagers – and then gone.
Leaving in a balance of suppressed tears,
as I still leave now, with every goodbye,
in the entropic embers of our flickering years.

TRANSIENT EQUATIONS OF LAWS & LIES

There was certainly no love in a town with no truth.

Years later, I returned to my home town.
The streets and houses were intrinsically the same,
but the people were different
and the language was different,
and the atmosphere bore a mood
of transience and blame.
Yet the people and the language
and the mood they spoke in
did the same things these streets
were obliged to do:
they drove the same cars around the same corners
and bought the same ice cream from similar shops.
These streets had changed hands for the sake of collateral,
and offered glittering beads in the deception of returns.

Determined hands owned everything then,
in this new culture of old and ancient races.
It was a transposing mythology,
built over the eyelids of children;
a slight of hand, imposing the greed of nations.
It was a ploy to loosen the stubborn authority
of inherited wealth into pirate pockets.

The ancients were told they were uncomfortable here,
and when questioned about guilt, were afraid to speak.
They were confused by the displacement of devalued lives,

while alien governments peered from blind windows.

It was time for the song of new customers now –
those who subscribed to the globalist creed,
knee deep in money and laundered blood –
a distilled and mesmerising no-man's land.

There was certainly no love in a town without truth;
that bore no responsibility to the value of its past.
And in an effort to stabilise the fragile plot
it was soon protected by judicial bonds.
These were built of corruptible words,
withholding the fortune of blatant lies.
They were devised to curb protest
or negative comment,
as well as the yearning for justified rebellion.

In the end – and feeling more than excluded,
the ancients whispered treachery,
while running to the hills.
These fragmented families,
who thought heritage was infinite,
are now sweeping its dust off the edge of town.

BIODEGRADABLE CULTURES

via the imbalanced mask of schooled diversity.

If you let their laws inside your house,
via the imbalanced mask of schooled diversity,
they will override your tame proclamations
in the maze of their own religious doctrine.
They will attempt to roll out a second constitution,
while denouncing your justice, as the injustice of fools –
a colonising blasphemy; a sinful pollution.
You will be numbed by the intransigence
of their archaic tools.

SELF-MEDICATION

From the pharmacy of Druids.

I did not trust my absent doctor –
especially hearing rumours
he had finally left town.
So on feeling a sudden healing sensation,
I cancelled his prescription
from the pharmacy of Druids.
I then reported his actions
to the cynically appointed woke police,
who pulled down his bronze effigy
in the surgery's marbled lobby.
They felt it far beyond shameful
that he had failed his expected duty –
that of honouring his lawful contract
with a potentially dying patient;
albeit a noted hypochondriac –
who had sought to blur his symptoms
by including poverty and drama
in his list of valid ailments.
The woke police left looking smug
and in my opinion, pale and ill –
being short on required vitamins
for their Mother Hubbard remedies –
being guilty of true vitality
in their whims of knee-jerk justice.

HIS DEATH SHALL HAVE NO FOOTNOTE

Creased into threadbare, remembered folds.

I left no note to explain myself;
I would have nailed it to the sideboard, just to be sure.
To be sure it would not die, loose and lost,
inside the dry ribs of a smokey drawer –
a hermit of truth, nestling amongst dead things;
the old things that might yet have their say.

These fragments of lives a family stores,
the woven apprenticeships to allow their passing.
These treasures, well known, but discontinued,
are the fragile steps of our separate ways,
all united in this drawer of folly –
in this mood of surplus, forgotten malaise.
Hair-grips and compass, scattered to their poles,
with photographic negatives – blind without their prints.
And safety-pins, guarding aggressive springs;
and sealing wax – keeping the secrets of peace.
They gather a contradiction of welcome dust,
in these drawers of our almost continental corners.

Here, the soft angled motions of deliberation
have wound the wool, back into a ball.
And here, with the tourist snap of holiday maracas,
the cotton-threaded needles still sing through their weave.
And the dark glasses and the reading glasses –
no longer appropriate for sight or weather,

explore their own regions of scars and scratches,
that grow like life in a petri dish.
They mirror the wounds of human thinking,
drawn on the brain of surplus meditation,
as their lenses multiply these shaded contents
into all the secrets of a new astronomy.
They taunt the impurity of the three wheeled car
and the arm of a dead doll, with casual fingers.
There is a cube of pool chalk from the 1960s,
and a spent cigar tube, scented vaguely of August.
And see the red veins of a travelled map,
creased into threadbare, remembered folds –
now discarded with a liturgy of holy verse –
a hymn book, offered to seasonal souls:
its urge made keener by this dormant death.

The drawer is lined with newspaper from the streets,
with its brown fascinations of stained and stored words –
its date, holding fast in a rigid corner,
to fix a mystery to this era of nonsense.
It reflects a stiffness in the curve of a spoon,
and the disowned vanity of no-one's comb.

A future day will find unfocussed eyes,
lingering in the passing glance of a trusted patron –
they will own a moment of this scattered feast,

'His Death Shall Have No Footnote' continues...

armed with the mobility of lightbulbs and drawing pins.
A gaze that will one day define the full measure,
of rare commitment, holding to this captured truth –
and to my own brief words of lost farewell –
not nailed down, or spread apart –
as I am not nailed down or exalted in death.
I am merely ammunition for God's next great swipe –
to be slid, unremembered, into a popular drawer.

6
EPILOGUE

Apocalypse of Poverty or Just Me?

THE LAST ACT

In the broken landscape of his own dead children.

The pied piper invites us to meet the new Tsar,
in the broken landscape of his own dead children.
Eventually there is nothing to fight for anymore –
and it is time to release those brutalised minions.
Release them now – from this sacrificial death –
from the burden of dirt – both burial and goal.
Free the cast of conflict from your folly of ego.
Stop playing president in a true theatre of war.
Acting is a crude form of megalomania –
shouting its lines until everyone is killed.
Our leaders ask too much of a borrowed faith –
They are wretched children, loud but unskilled.

4th March 2022

APOCALYPSE OF POVERTY OR JUST ME?

...into a lunacy of liberalised delight

1

Is it the end, or is it me? Yes, I think it must be me.
No one else will say what they think –
trapped in a pc silence and a drought of ink.
Afraid to rock a boat that is sinking at the bow.
The Captain's hat has adorned his skeleton
for a long while now.

If you won't break the silence and save yourselves,
I am going overboard, alone.
And you will be on your own... in your many millions –
a faceless, nameless, ignoramus.
A servant of a pernicious swell –
lost in a medieval tide, lit by burning books.

We thought we had sailed west enough,
but a loathing clung on and dragged us back,
like the call of upset children might –
into a mercy – into the flight –
into a lunacy of liberalised delight,
where we were all to blame, except them –
they only had to work on their malady of spite.

We were egged-on by an alternative greed –
a corporate vice, that hooked us back;
that called us back to rumours of duty –

the weeping bill of monstrous fathers;
the mithering scourge of colonial massacres –
and thus enmeshed into a process of apology,
that of accepted new blood and brotherhood.

We had hauled these babies up too close,
presenting a fake and depleted bosom –
a pretend concern, completely in vain,
that sucked out our last breath with poison time.
It was night by then – our time to rest,
and while we slept they deleted the future –
for all of us – including them –
and for all the nations of willing inheritors.
They piled its technologies before reckless gods,
lighting the meltdown of a cleansing pyre.

Some had thought they could include the world
in private schemes of wealth and distaste –
just to take the edge off their nagging guilt
with the thinnest skin of benevolent love –

The slavery of paid-work –
caging the dove.

They set them to mine coal in the opaque dark,
or in the ruthless fields of burning heat –

'Apocalypse or Just Me?' continues...

or the gasping roots of soot and smoke,
and based on this English translation of progress,
they thought they could feed whole worlds with talk –
words that could barely feed a listening ear.
Yet just to be sure, they invited millions more –
to be a square peg in their rounded veneer.
It was a convenient and lucrative begging bowl.
They enlisted their children as symbols of poverty
and snapped their legs to make them pay.
Did they really think people would starve
if there was any other way?
The rich made scavengers of people that day,
in an attempt to release a pathetic guilt.

The world had never imagined, as a natural theme,
that though driven and hindered by the same hunger,
the wretched were minded to a new creed,
where, even with iPhones, they continue to be beggars.

2
We have charred our planet's heart.
We have exhausted every single part.
We cultivated death, like gardeners on the moon –
offering a plot of nothing more than dust –
nothing but grey – not even rust.
Maybe a future crop of coffee, held in trust?

There was no shortage of land, of course,
but it was never scheduled for human dreams.
In humankind's own mind, it is itself a disease –
even in the places it never wanted to be –
places where they even fought for the upper-hand,
as though it matters in total squalor,
who your leader might be.

There is salt for our wounds in the noble sea,
and I shall di(v)e there tomorrow, with any luck.
Let me sink into those ancient waters now,
and drown in its thick-headed gossip of muck –
that much more important, spreading space,
where, immersed in solution,
we are truly dead, but never quite abandoned
by the universal paste.

BY FLUKE

under an ocean of sky.

My rebellious nature
is tired of swimming.
I am diving deeper
and waving goodbye.
Like the fluke of a whale,
diving deep to discover
the nadir of the brim –
under an ocean of sky.

SLAVE SHIPS IN THE MEDITERRANEAN

So everything is going according to plan.

The slaves ferry themselves now,
crossing continents – with a promise of sweets.
Providing misery with lawless waves;
hoping for a 'human clause' in the justice of slavers,
who in reaching to soften their predecessors' guilt,
might offer the naïve promise of lighter tasks.

Slavers are keen to replace native classes
with these easier, cheaper and more pliable tools.
Their current residents seem too demanding,
having the right of refusal on working for nothing –
undermined as they are, by European bills.
To silence a betrayal, they are bribed with benefits –
so everything is going according to plan –
the huge, unstoppable fail.

They have bent the establishment into a fragile Arcadia –
raised above the ashes of European lives.
They want us to fight for our treasured roots,
while hoping none but new customers survive.
This is the wealth of the richest,
resting on the most gullible of the fittest;
A ploy, on which to build a false utopia,
on the unsteady platform of failing trust.

2015

THE RIGHT HAND OF LEFTIST BETRAYAL

It drags behind them like spilt entrails.

Weep for your nation – for it is truly forgotten.
The liberal-snake slithered in while you were at work.
It let the tyres down on your privileged existence,
with a self-satisfied hiss and a condescending smirk.
A sabotage informed by snake-talk in the long grass,
while leaning on the hatred of a forked tongue.
It was their broken version of the Trojan Horse –
an effigy of idealism – painted with hate;
or a relic growth, from the shadows of history –
built from the knotted wood of sulking trees.
With this they wove bridges of considerable charity,
that stretched into the most insidious dark.
Spanning without regard, the rumours of war –
and the truth of rape and genocide.
Misunderstanding the recoil of diversity,
with its conflicting factions and hell-bent religion,
whose cohorts chose to stride in all directions –
shoring the grievance of defensive ghettoes.

These are the subtle details naïve eyes cannot follow,
even with an altered history, bleeding from the shadows.
It drags behind them like spilt entrails,
talking to itself in the blind slur of marxism.
Nothing is sure or sacred to right facing liberals,
it is change for disruption's sake – nothing more.
Lest for the wind of their self-righteous idealism,

as though there is nothing already here to build upon.
They are hoping to shape a modest anarchy,
more conforming to their unfounded frame –
a square peg, forced into thoughts of rounded souls –
each soul designated apportioned blame.

They are at the coast now removing the sea.
They are at the borders, with their reckless vanity.
Your flat tyres will not rush to stop their work,
as they welcome new friends to your expiring lives.
They placate the passage of the abused and vulnerable
with the condescending baggage of offered sweets.

DO NOT CONDEMN THE WORLD TO DARK

With the merciless glare of a darker light.

Without light, the economy of darkness will prevail.
Without darkness, light will burn itself out
and darkness will prevail.

We must believe in the balance of democracy, or fail.
We must believe in the right to speak our minds.

If you silence either truth or falsehood with petty laws,
they will prevail, and you will be caught
in the expedience of their lie.

If you douse the darkness with the pitch of your soul,
it will glow with light in the minds of others –
they will outshine your blight;
they will replace your endeavours
with the merciless glare of a darker light.

THE DEAD OF THE FIRST RACE WAR

A remembrance of the dead, returning in disguise.

There was of course, a trumpet call –
a proclamation of both courage and mourning;
a simultaneous and imperfect waver;
a deliberation of brass, upon its highest-edge.
And there was an expectant threat of failure –
resentful of rehearsed notes or chosen path.
It blew its tribute in spite of the trumpeter,
whose juggling to catch each underlying phrase,
was wind-assisted by agile lips –
playing for time around winter-white gloves –
and by the free-centring of a rogue mouthpiece;
a lip-distorted-quivering of ordered notes.
And all the time, emulating a blast from above –
a pitying admonishment, played on bright staves.
And with the toy eyes of soldiers, spent in glory,
that refused to be blinded by a prouder sorrow.
And by a blurred rain of chastising poppies,
descending from above, in mind and memory;
a remembrance of the dead, returning in disguise.

We shuffled down the high street then, in boot silence.
Heading for the Cenotaph,
where old wars still churn the ground,
and where our last battle had been fought, man on man;
where we had broken each other into extinguished hearts,
until there was no colour left, but red.

'The Dead of the First Race War' continues...

There was an easy silence then – an understanding –
that although we were still tribally segmented,
we were all the same race – black and white –
we had fought beside each other's face,
and there was some element of tampering religion
that had blindly urged us on – or a stoked idealism,
or a jealousy, embedded in the misreading
of our cultural song.
It had seemed (only to simple minds)
to be as easy as the space between our colour.

Finally, we all shook hands
and prepared to return to our various ghettos –
places where diversity still failed to explain its true heart.
It seemed a stuck umbrella that refused to open;
a stunted flower, that might have been,
were the unveiling fingers of the bud
not failed, usurped or broken.

Even so, we walked as one,
like cut-out people, unfolded from paper –
just as we were once all made of Sun.

We were joined at the hand by some mysterious blade
that had scissored our shape to fit a peaceful future –
a time that might prove the most challenging crusade –

where words beyond mere effort, needed to be spoken,
while seeking to unravel the tribal tether –
in that basic need of acknowledgement and freedom.

Most of us walked with a limp by then,
and with a fragile expression of universal understanding.
Clutching photographs of our needless dead,
now bound in the quiet glory of golden thread.
These men and women had all contrived
to resemble one another in piteous death –
and had no compass now to aim their weapons,
in spite of race or colour or accented breath.
They stared beyond timeless squares, with hollow eyes,
now armed with a faithful, sympathetic gaze.
They had seen the inevitability of a resentful war –
always coming, yet with suitable surprise;
the media, in its badgering folly
had stirred the pot too thick, too long and too wide.

We shuffled on – all maintaining it was the will of God
and that God had won – that god of dread.
A god, that in the end, suits everyone –
when everyone is one way or another, dead.

THE FINAL NOTE OF THE ARTIST

Sometimes, we can see the distances.

Are we ghosts, destined to remain unknown,
except unto ourselves?
We rally about our careful thoughts,
but none know the twists and turns
that brought us here, or why.
Or even where to go,
beyond this pliable framework of bone and spirit.
Sometimes, we can see the distances
that call us on to paint our sign –
to name things – and get this life of labelling done –
to move the mountain above the blackened sun
and explore the sea – to see beyond its edge of sky...
but their has to be an end and that becomes the why?
Yes, that becomes the afterglow
when our light has shone.
In a moment, I will leave my brush for others to use,
washed almost clean in the artist spirit...
but there will be a residue of something still to come –
a fractured prism of new and understated light.
I will walk the path to silence then,
having written this down for other ears.
Not a map of guidance or a hand in the abyss,
but merely a confession, handed through the years
that may still have some illuminating spark?
Or a simple note of comradeship and shared ideals –
God speed, good luck, goodbye. Try not to be too dark.

Milton Keynes UK
Ingram Content Group UK Ltd.
UKHW040400111224
452348UK00004B/312